Wallpaper

A Collection of Modern Prints

Charlotte Abrahams

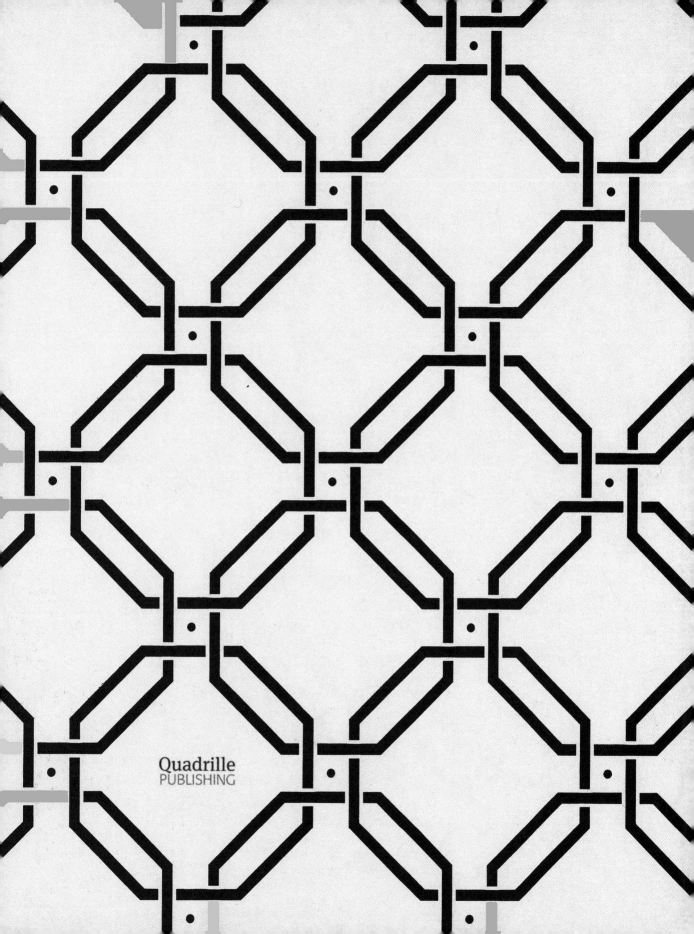

Quadrille
PUBLISHING

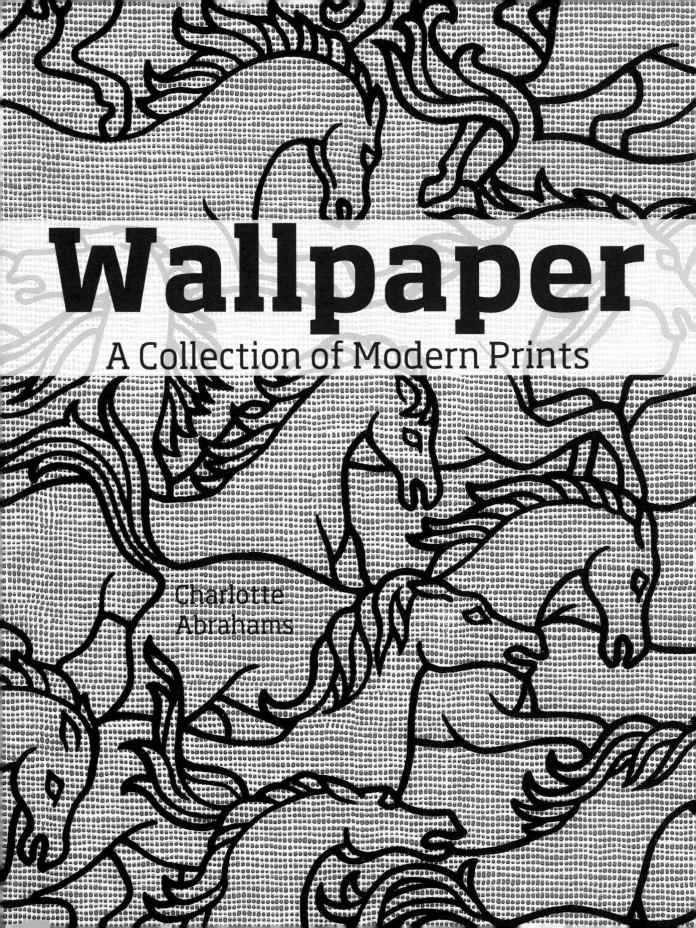

Wallpaper

A Collection of Modern Prints

Charlotte
Abrahams

Editorial Director: **Anne Furniss**
Project Editor: **Lisa Pendreigh**
Assistant Editor: **Romilly Morgan**
Art Director: **Helen Lewis**
Designer: **Lucy Gowans**
Picture Researcher: **Liz Boyd**
Design Assistant: **Katherine Cordwell**
Production Director: **Vincent Smith**
Production Controller: **Aysun Hughes**

First published as *Wallpaper: The Ultimate Guide* in 2009
This edition first published in 2013
Quadrille Publishing Ltd
Alhambra House
27–31 Charing Cross Road
London WC2H 0LS
www.quadrille.co.uk

British Library Cataloguing-in-Publication Data
A catalogue record for this book is available from the British Library.

ISBN 978 184949 357 4

Printed in China

This book has been
printed in Hexachrome,
an advanced printing
process that uses six
component colours rather
than the conventional four.
While Heachrome* offers over
3,000 controllable colours, there are
still some limitations and variations within
the printing process. As a result, it is impossible to
guarantee the fidelity of the colours reproduced. It is
important to note that different batches of wallpaper from
any manufacturer will vary minutely in colour. When buying
wallpaper, always check the batch numbers on the roll and buy from
the same batch whenever possible.

For George, Hamish and Paddy,
with love and thanks.

Contents

Introduction
A Brief History of Wallpaper

The story of wallpaper is one of fluctuating fortunes. 20 years ago, 80 years ago, 140 years ago, papered walls were beyond passé; today, as in the 18th Century, they are the last word in decorative chic. All fashions are cyclical, but wallpaper's continual resurgence can be put down to two things: technical innovations and – more importantly – our innate desire to decorate the walls which surround us.

The first major breakthrough was the arrival of wallpaper rolls towards the end of the 17th century. Although wallpaper had been used as a decorating device since the 16th century, the size of the sheets (a mere 30 x 36cm) had meant it was more suited to lining chests than hanging on walls. The discovery that single Dominos (as the sheets were known) could be joined together to form something long enough to cover a wall was revolutionary.

The next significant development occurred at the start of the 18th century. Up until then, wallpaper had been turned into rolls after printing which meant that pattern repeats could be no larger than the old Domino sheets. Technological improvements meant that the process could now be reversed, giving designers access to a canvas 12 times the size.

The arrival of large scale repeats heralded a golden age for wallpaper. Designers embraced it as a new art form and consequently the aristocracy, who had always derided wallpaper as a poor man's answer to tapestry and wood panelling, began to see it as a desirable product in its own right. Lavishly papered walls became the height of fashion.

However, as the 19th century dawned, it became clear that if the burgeoning wallpaper industry was to flourish, it had to find a way of making paper more affordable. The first commercially successful wallpaper printing machine was patented in Britain in 1839 by Potters & Ross. Aesthetically, the results were poor compared with hand blocked papers but what the new, machine-printed papers lacked in quality was more than made up for in quantity. In 1834, for example, the British wallpaper industry produced 1.2 million rolls. By 1851, a decade after the

first machine-printed papers went on sale, output had rocketed to 5.5 million rolls and the cost to the consumer had been slashed. What was once a luxury item could now be picked up by anyone with sixpence to spare.

Machine printing also had a profound effect on the designs that could be used: hand blocking had produced rich colours, but machines allowed for unrivalled detail. In France, this sparked a craze for trompe l'oeil, while in Britain, mechanisation led to papers covered with flowers so realistic they appeared three-dimensional.

Not everyone welcomed wallpaper's cheap, super-real new world. Design reformers such as A.W.N Pugin and his successor Owen Jones, believed lower prices meant lower standards and that such naturalistic motifs were ill-suited to interior walls. Wallpaper, they claimed, should feature either Gothic architectural motifs or the Arts and Crafts Movement's stylised florals. The fashion cognoscenti took note and wallpaper fell from grace.

Its survival through the 20th century can be attributed almost entirely to the mass market. There were brief flurries of interest from the design world (in the 1950s for example, American company Schumacher worked with Frank Lloyd Wright, while in Britain, Sanderson produced an abstract collection aimed specifically at architects) but for most of the century, the industry concentrated on turning out paper that was cheap, easy to clean and easy to hang.

By the late 1990s even the mass market had begun to eschew papered walls in favour of minimal paint. However, just as wallpaper reached its nadir, a new generation of designers emerged who seemed determined to reinvent it for the new millennium. People such as Brit-based designers Sharon Elphick and Deborah Bowness who used digital technology to produce the kind of statement-making feature wallpaper not seen since the French panoramics of the late 19th century.

Two decades on wallpaper is enjoying a sustained renaissance. There are papers referencing – and sometimes precisely replicating – every historical style from flock and photo-real scenics to Chinoiserie and Toile de Jouy and they're available at prices to suit every budget. This book is a visual celebration of some of those designs. Enjoy.

Chapter 1

Architectural Illusions

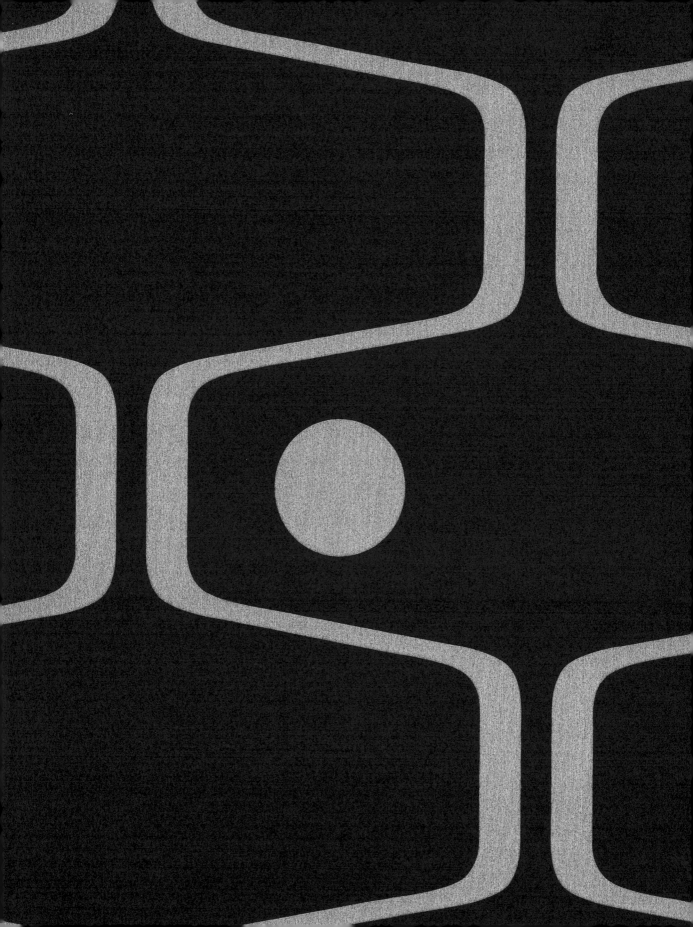

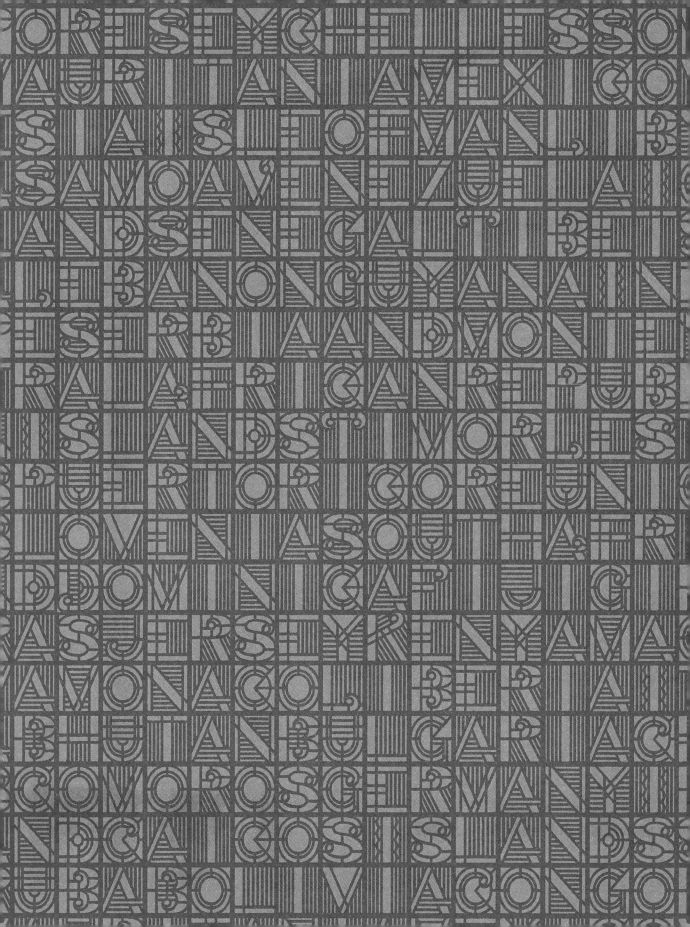

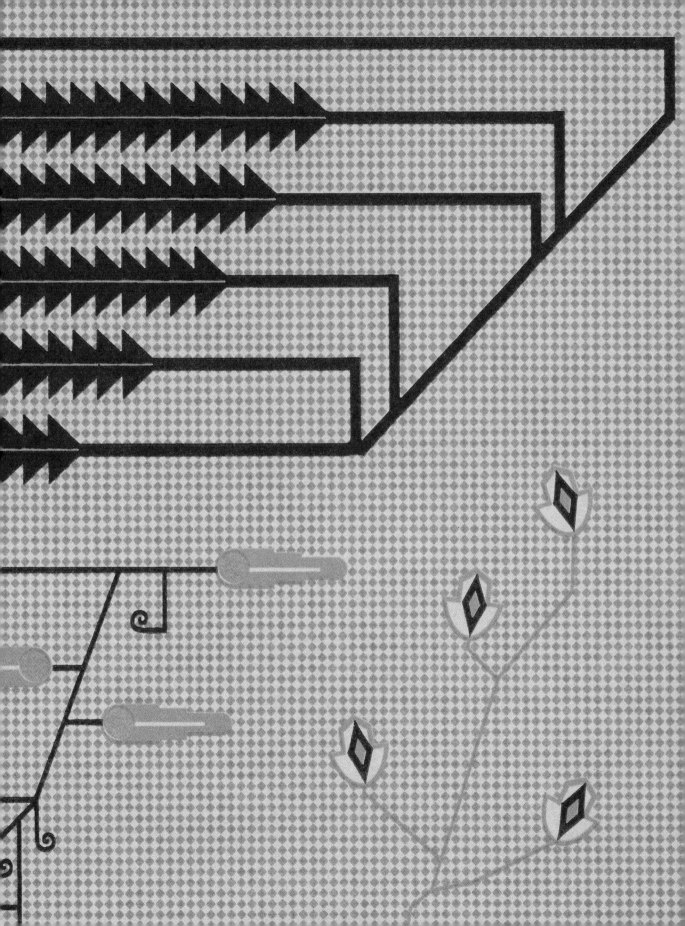

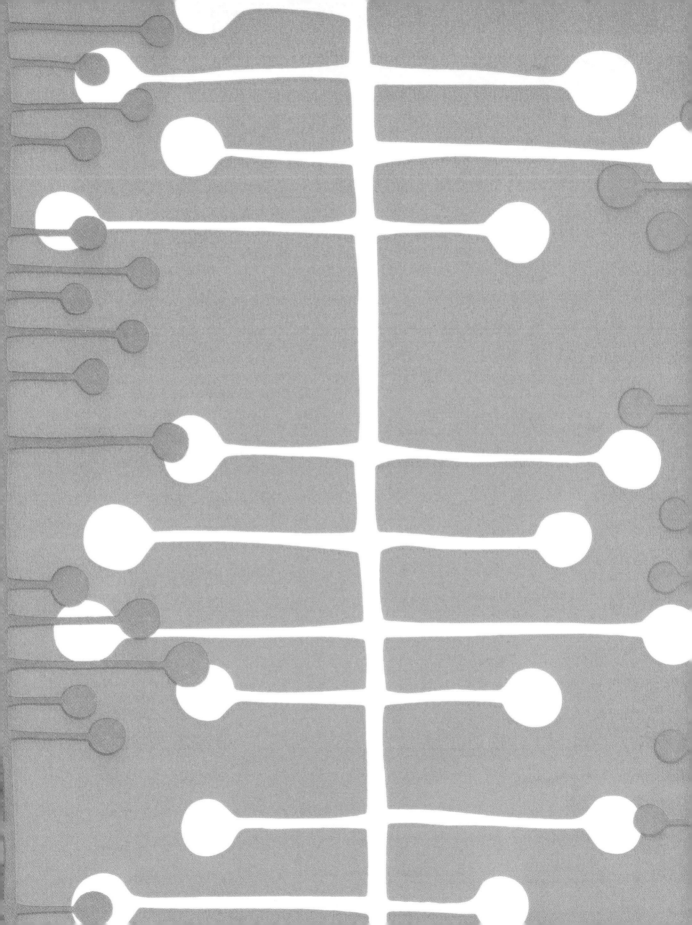

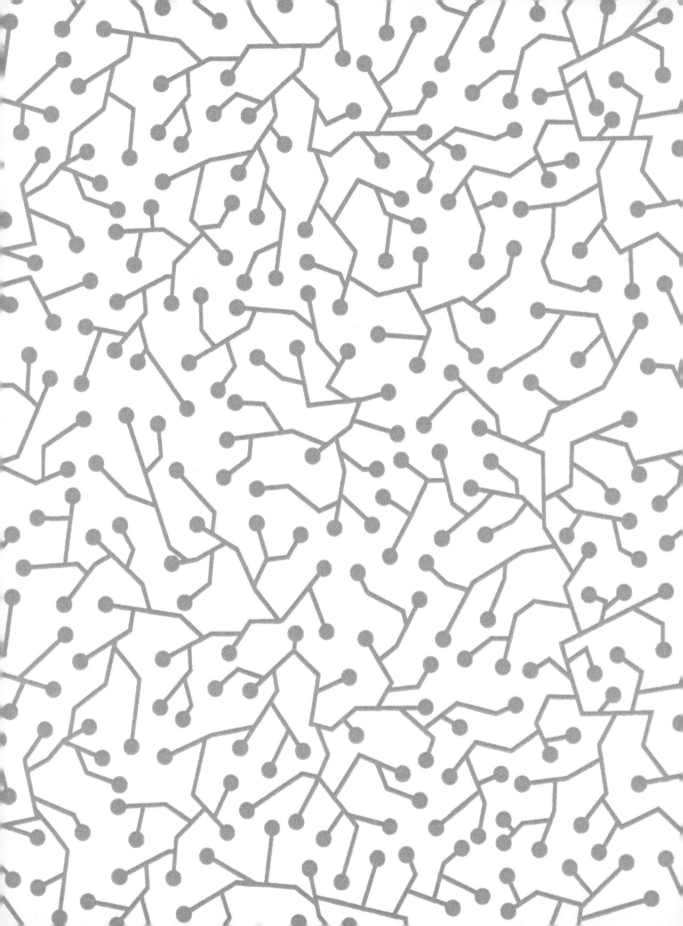

Fabulous Florals

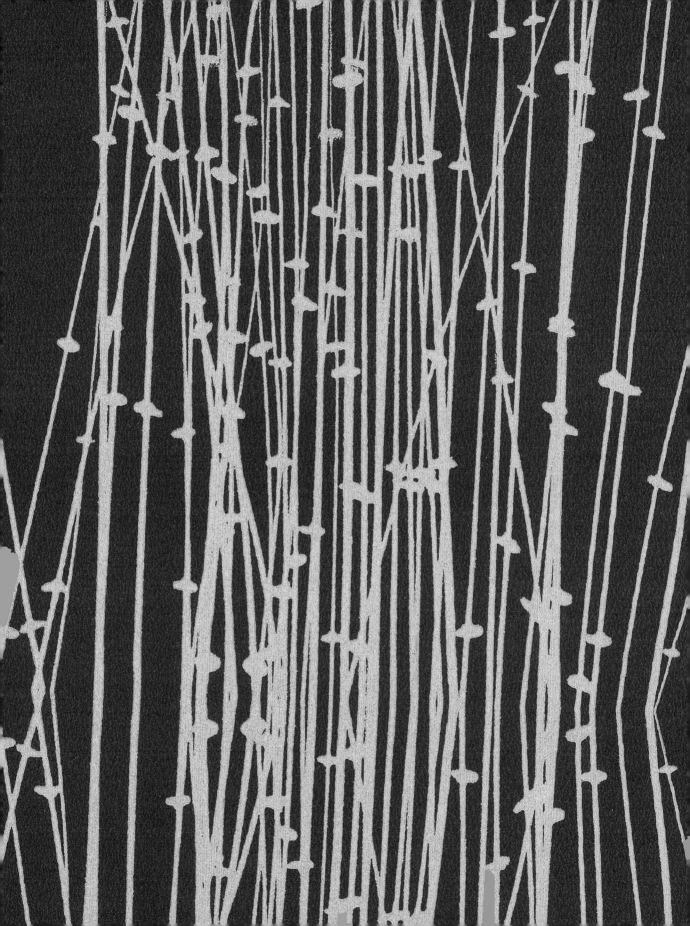

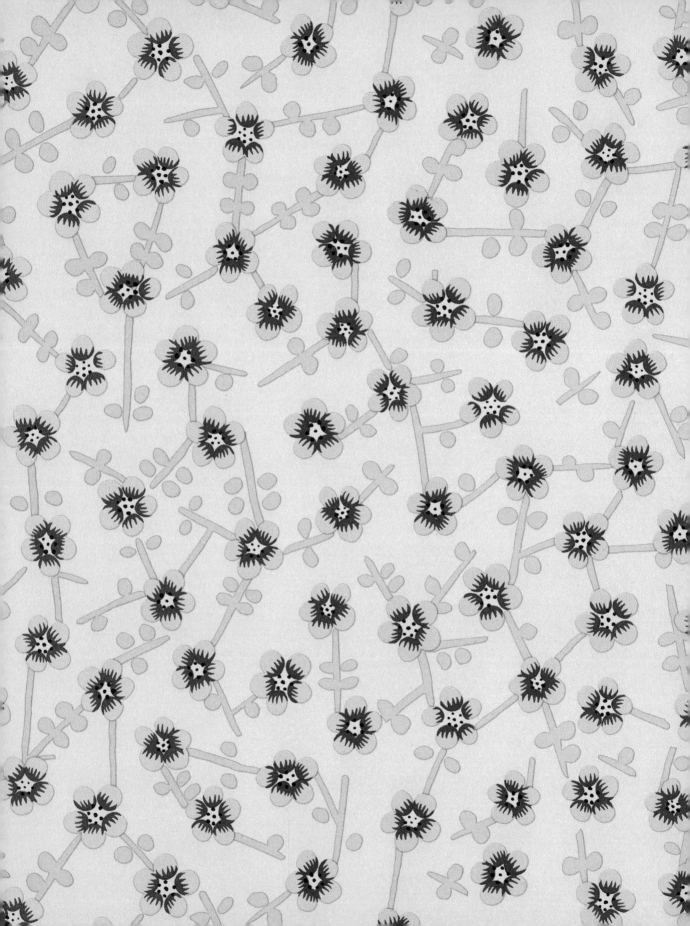

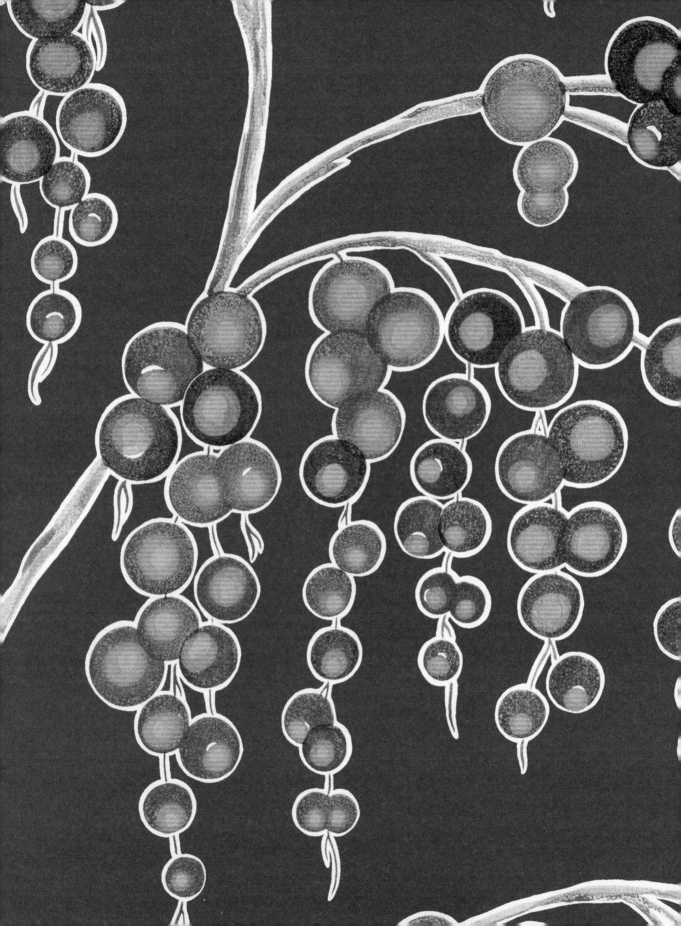

Pasted Pictures

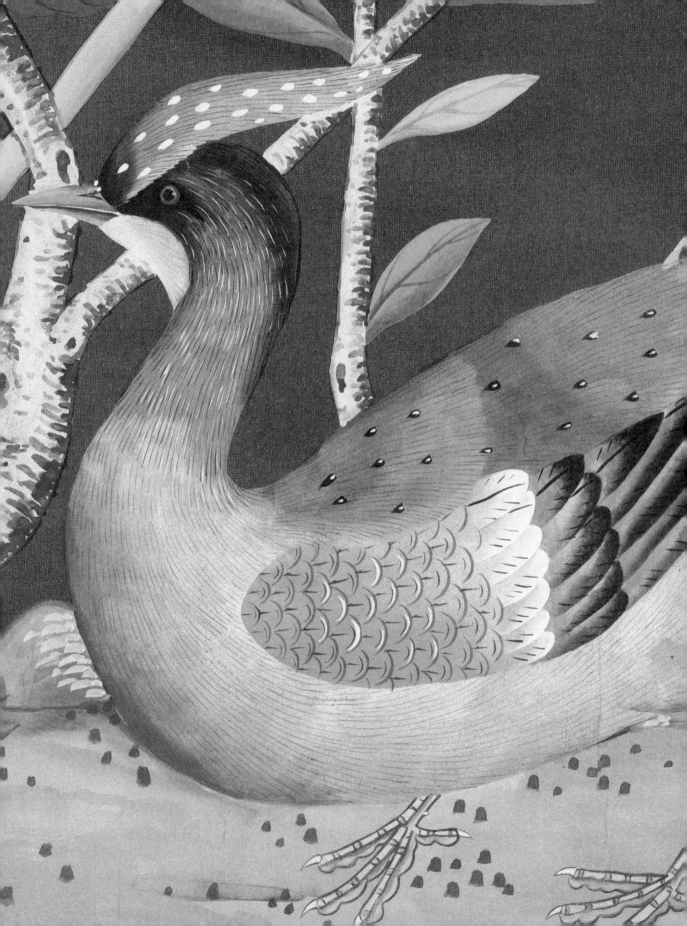

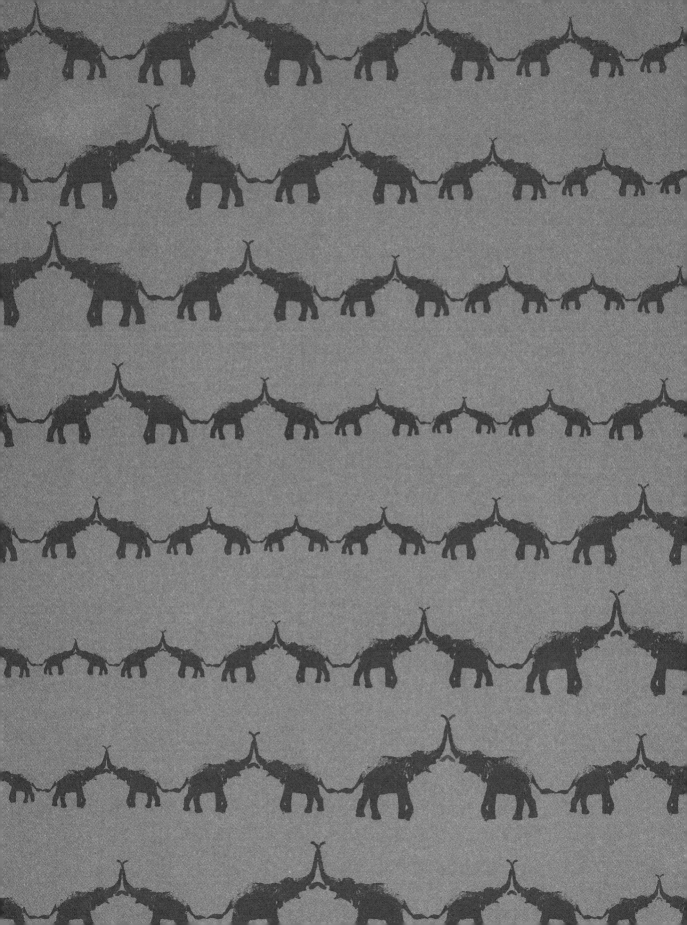

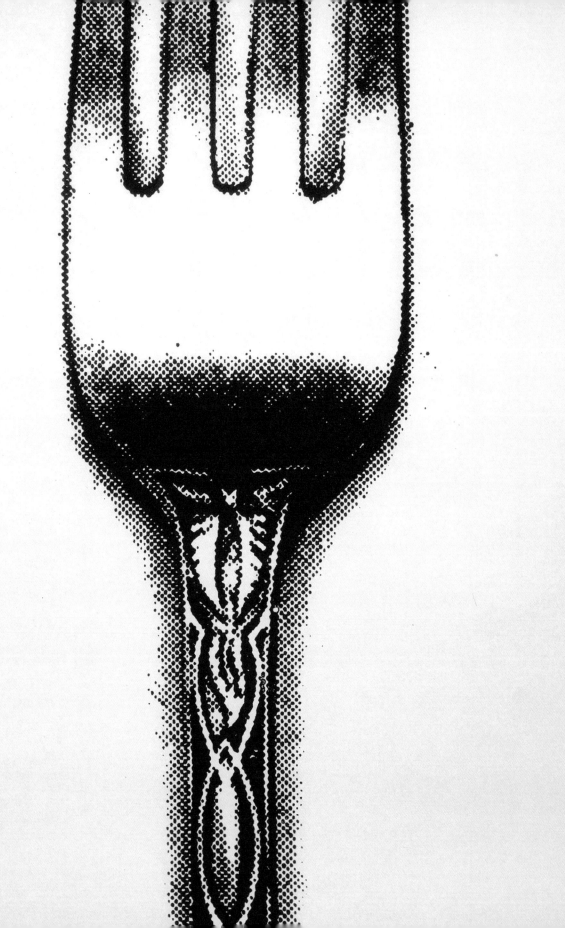

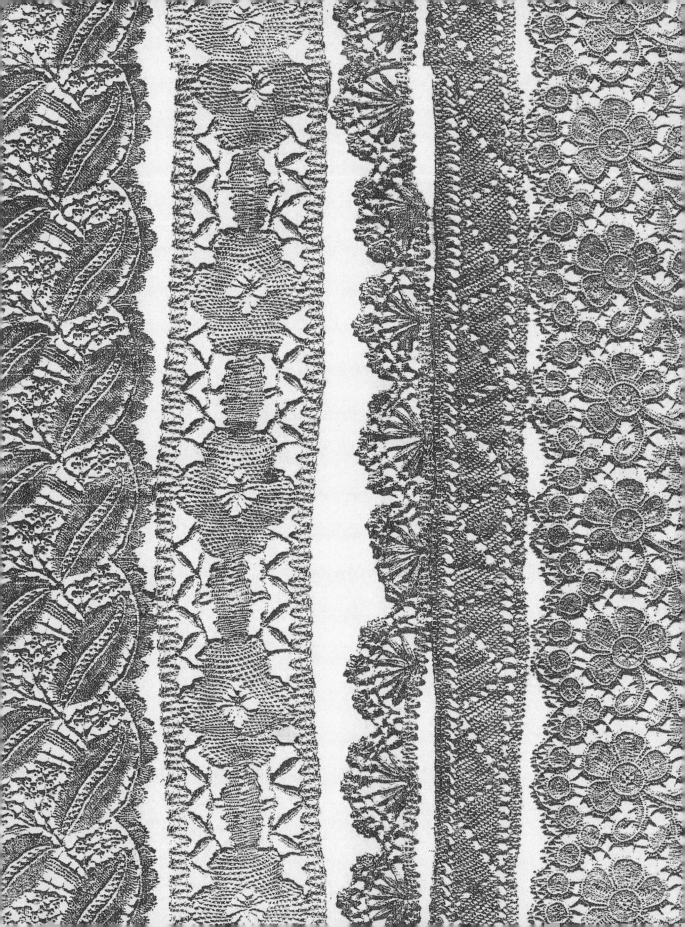

Index of Wallpapers

Lizzie Allen
'Jazz in Central Park' in Spring
Website: lizzieallen.co.uk

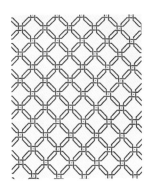

**Barbara Barry
for Kravet**
'Chic Link Net'
Website: barbarabarry.com/
kravet.com

**Florence Broadhurst
for Signature Prints**
'Horses Stampede'
Website: signatureprints.com.au

Fromental
'Nonsuch' in Unconscious Style on
Moongold Silk
Website: fromental.co.uk

Tracy Kendall
'In the White Room'
Website: tracykendall.com

Harlequin
'Contour' from the Virtue
Collection
Website: harlequin.uk.com

Sally Hemphill
'Clapper'
Website: govindiahemphill.com

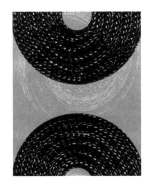

Élitis
'Opium' from the Tenue de Soirée
Collection
Website: elitis.fr

Cole & Son
'Albany Damask Flock' from the
Classix Exotic Flock Collection
Website: cole-and-son.com

Anya Larkin
'Artemis'
Website: anyalarkin.com

**Absolute Zero ° in
collaboration with the
Southbank Centre**
'Net and Ball' in Black
Website: southbankcentre.co.uk

Linda Florence
'Digital Flock Morphic Damask'
Website: lindaflorence.me.uk

Maya Romanoff
'Mother of Pearl' in Fire Coral
Website: mayaromanoff.com

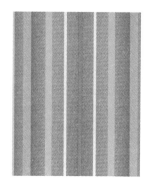

Harlequin
'Alta' from the
Arkona Collection
Website: harlequin.uk.com

Madison & Grow
'Estella' in Berkshires on
Parchment from the
Pasadena Collection
Website: madisonandgrow.com

**Sydney Albertini
for Studio Printworks**
'Byzantium' in Leander
Website: studioprintworks.com

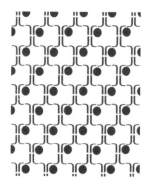

**Given Campbell for Studio
Printworks**
'Pipes' in Hinson
Website: studioprintworks.com

Larsen
'Couture' in Jasper
Website: larsenfabrics.com

Larsen
'Backdrop' in Peppercorn
Website: larsenfabrics.com

Lambert
'Muna' in Black
Website: lambert-home.de

Jane Churchill at Colefax and Fowler
'Dorset' in Granite from the Grovepark Collection
Website: janechurchill.com

Tres Tintas
'Ondas'
Website: trestintas.com

Romo
'Laurito Flock' in Ebony
Website: romo.com

Extratapete GmbH
'Lui' 01
Website: extratapete.de

Extratapete GmbH
'Anna'
Website: extratapete.de

Brian Yates
'Odeon'
Website: brian-yates.co.uk

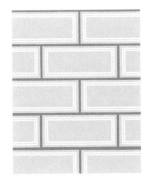

**Basso & Brooke
for Graham & Brown**
'Globe' in Cocoa
Website: grahambrown.com

Arte distributed by Brian Yates
'14203' from the Zenobia
Website: brian-yates.co.uk

Studio Printworks
'Le Temple des Grec' in Bastille
Website: studioprintworks.com

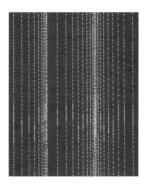

Andrea Pößnicker distributed by Arte
'Lady Light' in Silver Metallic on Kohl Black from the Pomp Collection

Andrea Pößnicker distributed by Arte
'Bricks' in Extra Virgin White Foam on Flashy Neon Pink

Maya Romanoff
'Komodo Vinyl Type II' in Willow
Website: mayaromanoff.com

Nobilis
'Darnier Noyer Fonce'
Website: nobilis.fr

Omexco distributed by Brian Yates
'LAA101' from the Laguna Collection
Website: brian-yates.co.uk

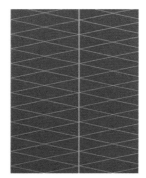

Natasha Marshall for Today Interiors
'Bridge' in Berry from the Graphic Collection
Website: todayswallpapers.com

Natasha Marshall for Today Interiors
'Billow' in Twilight
Website: todayswallpapers.com

Dedar
'Alhambra' in Quesi Nero
Website: dedar.com

Tres Tintas
'Espiga'
Website: trestintas.com

Tracy Kendall
'In the White Room'
Website: tracykendall.com

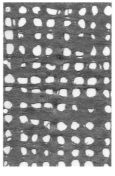

Sahco
'Oracle'
Website: sahco.com

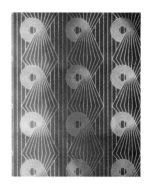

Erica Wakerly
'Mini Spiral' in Black/Silver
Website: printpattern.com

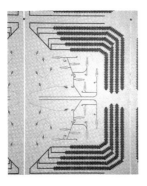

Neisha Crosland
'Donegal Palm' in Black Rose
Website: neishacrosland.com

Romo
'Tamino' in Fuchsia
Website: romo.com

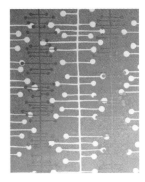

Miss Print
'Muscat' in Yellow
Website: missprint.co.uk

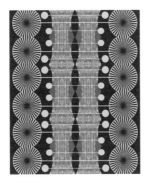

ATA Designs
'Trees'
Website: atadesigns.com

Hugh Dunford Wood
'Chevron' in Gatenby
Website: handmadewallpaper.co.uk

Andrew Hardiman for Kuboaa
'Allumette' in Broad Bean
Website: kuboaa.co.uk

Harlequin
'Contour' from the Virtue
Collection
Website: harlequin.uk.com

Harlequin
'Vigour' in Silver on Black from
the Virtue Collection
Website: harlequin.uk.com

Phillip Jeffries
'Spring' from the Seasons
Leaf Collection
Website: phillipjeffries.com

Cole & Son
'Haddon Hall' in White on
Silver from Classic Exotic Flock
Collection
Website: cole-and-son.com

**Manuel Canovas
for Colefax and Fowler**
'Cassis' in Fuchsia
Website: manuelcanovas.com

Graham & Brown
'Buckingham' from the
Superfresco Paintable Collection
Website: grahambrown.com

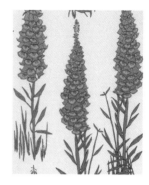

**Suzy Hoodless for Osborne &
Little**
'Foxglove' from the Hothouse
Collection
Website: osborneandlittle.com

Abigail Borg
'Polka Polka'
Website: abigailborg.co.uk

Sanderson
'Dandelion Clocks' in Chaffinch
Website: sanderson-uk.com

Clarissa Hulse
'Dragonfly' in Pewter on
Neon Pink
Website: clarissahulse.com

Clarissa Hulse
'Reeds' in Turquoise on Chocolate
Website: clarissahulse.com

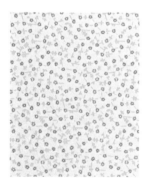

Designers Guild
'Primrose Hill' in Pink on
Turquoise
Website: designersguild.com

Designers Guild
'Maddalena' in Silver and Gold
on Black
Website: designersguild.com

Jill Malek
'Sleeping Briar Rose' in Noir
Website: jillmalek.com

**Florence Broadhurst
for Signature Prints**
'Tropical Floral'
Website: signatureprints.com.au

Jocelyn Warner
'Treetops' in Silver Grey
Website: jocelynwarner.com

Nina Campbell for Osborne & Little
'Famille Rose'
Website: osborneandlittle.com

Rachel Kelly
'Long Flower' in Coral and Stone and Lustre
Website: interactivewallpaper.co.uk

Timorous Beasties
'Thistle' in Black on Ivory from the Superwide Collection
Website: timorousbeasties.com

Timorous Beasties
'Thistle' in Silver on Ivory from the Superwide Collection
Website: timorousbeasties.com

Henry Wilson for Osborne & Little
'Maharani' from the Sariskar Collection
Website: osborneandlittle.com

Nancy Burgess for Studio Printworks
'Grand Pauline' in Golden Age
Website: studioprintworks.com

Fromental
'Chinon' in Cook
Website: fromental.co.uk

Claire Coles
'Garden Scene 1'
Website: clairecolesdesign.co.uk

Studio Printworks
'Fern' in Villa
Website: studioprintworks.com

**Manuel Canovas
at Colefax and Fowler**
'Clara' in Argent
Website: manuelcanovas.com

Watts of Westminster
'Percival' in Cardinal Graphite
Website: watts1874.co.uk

Farrow & Ball
'St Antoine' in Blue on Grey
Website: farrow-ball.com

Lorca for Osborne & Little
'Cattleya'
Website: osborneandlittle.com

Lorca for Osborne & Little
'Ninfa'
Website: osborneandlittle.com

Lorca for Osborne & Little
'Imperia'
Website: osborneandlittle.com

Kirk Brummel
'Boca Chica – Positive' in Red
on White
Website: brunschwig.com

**Billy McCarthy for Kirk
Brummel**
'Luxuriants Tracery' in Brown on
Cream from In Search of Unicorns
Collection
Website: brunschwig.com

Lim & Handtryck
'Höst' in Black on White
from the Funkis Collection
Website: limohandtryck.se

William Morris for Sanderson
'Fruit' in Coral Beige
Website: william-morris.co.uk

William Morris for Sanderson
'Golden Lily' in Pale Biscuit
Website: william-morris.co.uk

Tyler Hall
'First Bloom' in Snow Bud
Website: tyler-hall.com

Tyler Hall
'Kensington Gardens'
Website: tyler-hall.com

Tyler Hall
'Belgravia'
Website: tyler-hall.com

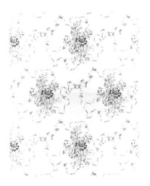

**Barbara Barry
for Kravet**
'In Bloom' in Chocolate
Website: barbarabarry.com/
kravet.com

The Silk Gallery Ltd
'Bouquet and Ribbon' in Blue
Ribbon and Coral Flower
Website: thesilkgallery.com

Josef Frank for Svenskt Tenn
'Krysantemer' in Yellow
Website: svenskttenn.se

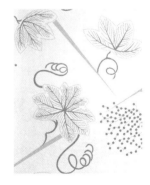

Emery & Cie
'Herbes Folles'
Website: emeryetcie.com

Miss Print
'Saplings' in Gold on Turquoise
Website: missprint.co.uk

Neisha Crosland
'Currant Leaf' in Polar
Website: neishacrosland.com

Neisha Crosland
'Firework Flowers' in Moss Pink
Website: neishacrosland.com

Natasha Marshall for Today Interiors
'Bloom' in Gold
Website: todaywallpapers.com

Harlequin
'Iola' in Hot Pink from
the Arkona Collection
Website: harlequin.uk.com

The Little Greene Paint Co
'Great Ormond Street' in
Verditure
Website: littlegreene.com

Madison & Grow
'Eloise' in Leaves at Night
Website: madisonandgrow.com

Harlequin
'Florian' in Gold on Black from
the Arkona Collection
Website: harlequin.uk.com

Harlequin
'Kimiko' from the Tamika
Collection
Website: harlequin.uk.com

David Oliver
'Mazurka' in Chocolate con Gusto
from the Orchestration Collection
Website: paintlibrary.co.uk

David Oliver
'Opium' in Sugar Pink
from the Liberation Collection
Website: paintlibrary.co.uk

Ella Doran
'Sunlight Through Leaves'
Website: elladoran.co.uk

Geoff McFetridge for Pottok
'All of Us'
Website: pottokprints.com

Geoff McFetridge for Pottok
'Little Whales'
Website: pottokprints.com

Geoff McFetridge for Pottok
'California Flowers'
Website: pottokprints.com

Inke Heiland
'Giraffe'
Website: inke.nl

Inke Heiland
'Vogeltjes'
Website: inke.nl

Charles Burger for Turnell & Gigon
'Ballon de Gonesse' in Jaune

Timorous Beasties
'London Toile' in Green
Website: timorousbeasties.com

Claire Coles
'Running Horses'
Website: clairecolesdesign.co.uk

GP&J Baker
'Songbird' in Multi on Gold from the Emperor's Garden Collection
Website: gpjbaker.com

Judit Gueth
'Koi' in Chinoiserie
Website: juditgueth.com

Judit Gueth
'Peacock' in Jade
Website: juditgueth.com

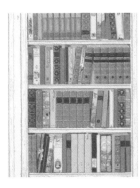

Richard Neas for Brunschwig & Fils
'Bibliotheque' in Multi
Website: brunschwig.com

ATA Designs
'City Series'
Website: atadesigns.com

Fromental
'Paradiso' in Ultramarine
Website: fromental.co.uk

Schumacher
'Chiang Mai Dragon' in Alabaster
Website: fschumacher.com

Pottok
'Apples Go Bananas'
Website: pottokprints.com

Hugh Dunford Wood
'Rousseau' in Fairground
Website: handmadewallpaper.co.uk

Absolute Zero °
'Tick-Tock' in Snow
Website: minimoderns.com

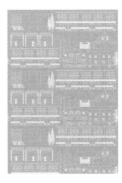

Absolute Zero °
'Do You Live in a Town?' in Milk Chocolate
Website: minimoderns.com

Belynda Sharples for The Art of Wallpaper
'Chickens'
Website: theartofwallpaper.com

Belynda Sharples for The Art of Wallpaper
'Countryside Toile'
Website: theartofwallpaper.com

Lizzie Allen
'Changing the Guards at Buckingham Palace' in Autum Gold
Website: lizzieallen.co.uk

Lizzie Allen
'London City Gents' in Autumn
Website: lizzieallen.co.uk

Lisa Bengtsson
'Familjen'
Website: lisabengtsson.se

Paul Loebach for Studio Printworks
'Yee-Ha!' in Agent Orange
Website: studioprintworks.com

Madison & Grow
'Erin' in Peacock on Shimmer
from the Pasadena Collection
Website: madisonandgrow.com

Absolute Zero °
'Sitting Comfortably?' in Snow
Website: minimoderns.com

Celia Birtwell
'Beasties' in Red on Oyster
Website: celiabirtwell.com

Ornamenta
'Doves' in Tea Rose on Champagne
from the Hand Printed Concept
Collection
Website: ornamenta.co.uk

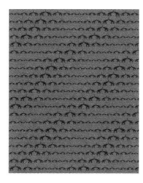

Jill Malek
'Baby Elephant Walk' in Red
Saffron
Website: jillmalek.com

Florence Broadhurst for Signature Prints
'Egrets'
Website: signatureprints.com.au

Schumacher
'Aviary' in Multi on White
Website: fschumacher.com

Louise Body
'Erotica' in Black on White
Website: louisebody.com

Marthe Armitage
'Jungle Birds' in Black
Website: hamiltonweston.com

Garin for Brian Lawrence
'Wallpaper Toile'
Website: brianlawrence.net

Cath Kidston
'Boat' in White
Website: cathkidston.co.uk

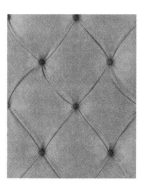

Endless Wallpaper
'Capitonné' in Green
Website: tapeten-bordueren.com

Mod Green Pod
'Butterfly Jubilee'

Tracy Kendall
'Fork' from the Eat Collection
Website: tracykendall.com

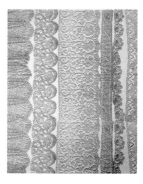

Louise Body
'Marney's Lace' in Charcoal
Website: louisebody.com

Ella Doran
'Stacks and Stripes'
Website: elladoran.co.uk

Ella Doran
'Sunlight Through Leaves'
Website: elladoran.co.uk

Marthe Armitage
'Manor House' in Dark Green
Website: hamiltonweston.com

Endless Wallpaper
'Paradise Lila' (one of four panels)
Website: tapeten-bordueren.com

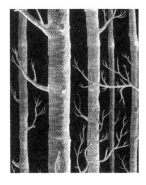

de Gournay
'North American River Views'
handpainted wallpaper
Website: degournay.com

Osborne & Little
'Best in Show' in Black on White
from the Walk in Park Collection
Website: osborneandlittle.com

Cole & Son
'Woods' from the Contemporary
II Collection
Website: cole-and-son.com

Dominic Crinson
'Londonscape' from the Murals
Collection
Website: crinson.com

Piero Fornasetti for Cole & Son
'Mediterranea' from
The Fornasetti Collection
Website: cole-and-son.com